Lucy Star @ 13

Let's Celebrate Trans and Gender Diversity

By   Kate Downey

Balboa Press books may be ordered through booksellers or by contacting:

Balboa Press
A Division of Hay House
1663 Liberty Drive
Bloomington, IN 47403
www.balboapress.com
1 (877) 407-4847

ISBN: 978-1-5043-1032-1 (sc)
ISBN: 978-1-5043-1031-4 (e)

Print information available on the last page.

Balboa Press rev. date: 09/28/2017

BALBOA
PRESS
A DIVISION OF HAY HOUSE

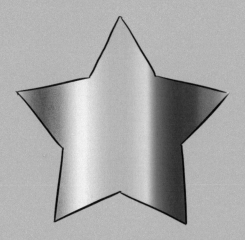

Let's celebrate trans and gender diversity

For Kate Stedman and Jenni Mitchell
for their love, friendship and interest in me
over many years

Hi it's Lucy here
I'm 13 now and so much has happened since I was 7.

Last year was the worst year of my life. It was a dark and lonely time for me. I just couldn't see a future. There were times when I thought about suicide.
If I couldn't be me I just didn't want to live.
There were times I couldn't talk to anyone the pain was so deep.
Sometimes I couldn't breathe.

I knew I was growing and I was so scared my body would grow to look like a man and I was terrified I would get a deep voice. I used to look at myself all the time in the mirror and I was so worried I'd look really masculine.

I experienced some really nasty comments from some of the kids at school.
One kid said to me Who are you? What are you?
Some days I just didn't go to school.

Mum and dad were incredibly worried about me.

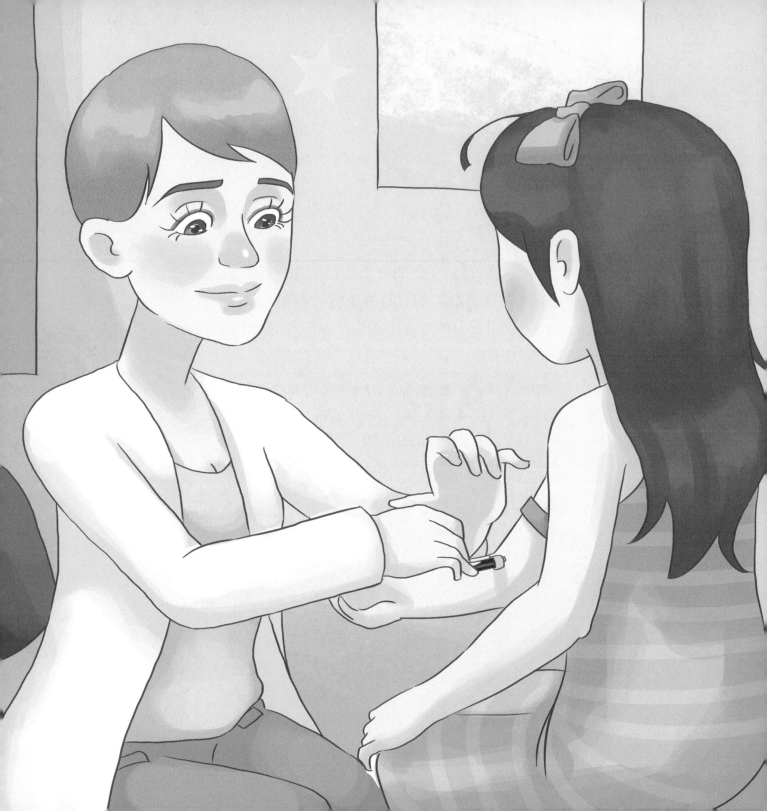

Seriously, if it wasn't for Dr Green - the Specialist at the Gender Centre at the Royal Children's Hospital I would have killed myself.

Dr Green talked to me about what I could do when the bullying occurred.
She taught me how to breathe. She also said I have to walk away and make sure I had my friends around me.

I also learnt I have to talk about how I feel rather than stay silent and bottle things up in my head.
Dr Green also explained to me that when trans children reach puberty around 12 years old they need to have puberty blockers (stage 1) of their treatment - it's medication to help them be who they really are.

Doctor Green took some blood tests and when I was ready for puberty she started me on the puberty blockers. Finally something was being done for me.

I take this medication now (it's an injection) every 3 months which prevents my body from developing into a male. I have to take this medication for about 3 years.

Dr Green said that during the 3 years I am on the blockers I can change my mind at any time and stop the treatment and there are no side effects... but I said no way... I am not changing my mind.

This year I started the puberty blockers and I feel so much better. I have hope that I can be me. I'm growing my hair which looks good.

When I turn 16 I will be ready to start oestrogen (stage 2) of my treatment. This will make my body look like a female body.

I still have to see lots of doctors but that's ok all my Clinicians are so supportive at the Gender Clinic.

When I am 18 I will be able to have surgery if I want to. Some people like me want to remove their penis and make it into a vagina. I'm not sure about this yet. I will see how I feel when I am older. Dr Green has been amazing and she always explains everything so I can understand what is happening. She also listens to me.

At school this year I decided I wanted to tell my year and the school about me. It was very important for me I just had to do it. Mum and dad were very supportive and Ms White the School Principal thought I was very brave.

But I said no I'm not brave this is just something I have to do. I'm not brave at all,
I just want people to know my story.

I want people to understand who I am.
I'm just a girl and there's nothing else to it.

Anyway last week I got up and told the school about me. I was
nervous but I wanted to do it.
Since then I have been really happy. Some kids are a bit mean and
they ask some funny questions but mostly everyone is great.

Maisie is still my best friend and I still see Marcel every weekend at our riding school.

He's going to Argentina next semester for 3 months to visit his dad's family in South America.

My new friends since starting high school are Matilda, Ruby, Hannah and Olivia.

I've also met an older student at my school called Max. He's in year 10 and we have a real bond. Max is transgender and he told me when he told his parents he was boy and he wanted to live as a boy his parents couldn't accept it. He said there were fights, arguments and they refused to talk about how he felt.

Max said his dad eventually left home and he hasn't seen him in 4 years. Max now lives with his aunt as his mum couldn't cope with Max's transition. Max said if it wasn't for his aunty he would have ended his life. We totally get each other.

Because of his aunt and the support he gets at school as well as his Doctor Max says life is so much better now. He feels free to be who he is.

I know he misses his mum and he is so hurt by his father but he's getting support. He's part of a LGBTI Youth Group that meets every month and he loves it.

My journey has in many ways been different to Max's as I have always had the support of my parents. That has made all the difference to me.

I have to tell you that Gingy died 2 years ago. It was really sad. I cried so much. We buried her in our backyard. I planted a garden over where we buried her and it is beautiful ... It's a really special place that I can go to and talk to her.
Meggie comes too...she really misses her...
Animals know so much. They are so intelligent.

Mum got us a new dog a golden retriever. He's so beautiful and lively. He's absolutely ruined Mum's garden. Mum tries to discipline him but she just ends up kissing him all over.
He is soooooo adoreable.

Dad's going to take him to puppy school.
He's starting next week.
Meggie's 14 now. She's so over Barry. He annoys her as he always wants to play with her.

Dad called him Barry after Barry Gibb of the Bee Gees. Mum wanted to call him Buddy but dad said he's a Barry. Dad plays the Bee Gees music all the time.

Mum is worried the neighbours will think she likes that music!

Mum's more into Joni Mitchell, Sade, Aretha Franklin and Adele.

My sister Bobbie is at university studying marketing and she has a boyfriend Dave.
Bobbie always tells me that she looks up to me!

Henry is studying Horticulture - he wants to be a landscape gardener.

I want to be a psychologist and help people like Dr Green does.

I just want everyone to understand that everyone has the right to be who they are...

It's that's simple!

Useful information

- » *LGBTI refers to - Lesbian, Gay, Bisexual, Transgender and Intersex*
- » *The number of trans children seeking treatment has risen in Australia and the USA.[1]*
- » *The Royal Children's Hospital Gender Clinic had one trans gender referral in 2003[2]*
- » *In 2016 there have been 226 referrals[3]*
- » *The reason for this increase is largely due to the support and medical treatment that children can receive now[4]*
- » *Dr Michelle Telfer at the Royal Children's Hospital believes that support around the world for trans children began about 15 years ago in the States and about 10 years ago in Australia*
- » *If trans and gender diverse people don't get the support they need 30% will attempt suicide and 50% will self-harm[5]*
- » *Hormone blockers (stage 1) are given to children when they are on the cusp of puberty*
- » *The medications, which suppress the body's production of estrogen or testosterone, essentially pause the changes that would occur during puberty.*
- » *That's really what these pubertal blockers do. They allow children who experience gender dysphoria the time and space to explore and settle on their gender identity.*

» *Children take these hormone blockers for about 3-4 years until they reach 16 years old.*

» *Stage 1 of the treatment - the suppression of puberty - is fully reversible.*

» *Stage 2 of the treatment - the administration of testosterone or oestrogen - has irreversible features. For testosterone use in females transitioning to males, these include hair growth, voice deepening and muscle growth. For oestrogen use in males transitioning to female, these include breast development, testicular shrinkage and growth height maturation.*

» *Before 2013 transgender children and their families had to go to Court in Australia to get approval for the treatment of puberty blockers (stage 1 and stage 2).*

» *But in 2013 that law changed - allowing children to get the treatment they needed without going to Court for Stage 1 treatment when they are 12 years old.*

» *The change in the 2013 law for stage 1 treatment is due to what has been referred to in subsequent cases, including Re: Jamie, as Gillick competency.[6]*

» *However, Adolescents still need to get Court approval to receive stage 2 of their treatment when they are 16 years old - this is being challenged at the moment with the hope that this law for stage 2 is reversed.*

Sources: 1-5 provided by Dr Michelle Telfer, Gender Clinic, Royal Children's Hospital, Melbourne

6 Gillick competency: is a term originating in England and is used in medical law to decide whether a child (under 16 years of age) is able to consent to his or her own medical treatment, without the need for parental permission or knowledge.

The Family Court of Australia has found that 15 year old "Jamie", the subject of the often-cited decision of the Full Court of the Family Court in Re: Jamie [2013] FamCAFC 110 (Re Jamie 2013), was competent to consent to the stage two treatment for gender dysphoria and authorised her to make her own decision in relation to that treatment. This case is one of many being heard by the Family Court following the decision in Re Jamie 2013 that whilst court authorisation is unnecessary for stage one treatment for gender dysphoria, the nature of stage two treatment requires the Court to determine the child's "Gillick competence" to make the decision.

Acknowledgements and thanks to

Associate Professor Michelle Telfer, Royal
Children's Hospital, Melbourne
Chilwell Library, Geelong
Geelong Library and Heritage Centre
John Allan
Juanita Barnes
Catherine D'Andria
Darren Grayson
John Howlett
Keri Koutsomitis

GENDER IS HERE
- - - - - - - - - - - - - - - - - -
NOT HERE

Authors note

Kate Downey lives in Geelong. This is her second book.

Kate wants people to understand the journey for transgender children especially when they reach puberty.

In this book Kate talks about the treatment children can receive for their body to grow into the gender as to who they identify as.

Before 2013 children and their families had to go to Court to seek approval for the puberty blockers (stage 1 and stage 2) of their treatment. This experience is not only costly and lengthy but extremely traumatic for both the child and families involved.

In 2013 that Court order was appealed and now all trans children can receive Stage 1 of this treatment without enduring any Court procedure.

Currently, in 2017, negotiations are taking place between the Family Court of Australia and Clinicians and Families for Stage 2 of the treatment to be available for children without going to Court.

Printed in the United States
By Bookmasters